ONE WEEK LOAN

TIME AND TIMELINES
IN THE PRIMARY SCHOOL

Pat Hoodless

Published by The Historical Association

Edited by   Emeritus Professor G.R. Batho

Prepared by   Marco Spinelli

The author would like to thank the following for permission to reproduce their materials:
Front cover illustration, Universal pocket sun and moon dial by Nicolas Rugendas, Augsburg, Germany, c. 1650, National Museums and Galleries on Merseyside
Figure 1, Beacon Press, Boston
Figure 5, Pictorial Educational Charts Trust
Figure 6, Soft Teach Educational
Figure 8, Picture 1 (Roman Fort) Ginn and Company Ltd. Pictures 3, 4 and 5 Longman Group.
Figure 9, Pictures 1 and 2 Longman group U.K.
Figure 15, Picture of Quetzalcoatl, Bellerophon Books, Santa Barbara
The author would also like to thank, for their advice in the preparation of the text, Professor Gordon Batho, Joan Blyth, Penelope Harnett and Nigel Hall, for assistance in the production of the timelines, Malcolm Hoodless and Richard Egan, and for examples of children's ideas from Stockton Heath County Primary School, Cheshire.

ISBN   0-85278-398-1

The Historical Association, founded in 1906, brings together people who share an interest in, and love for, the past. It aims to further the study and teaching of history at all levels: teacher and student, amateur and professional. This is one of over 100 publications available at very preferential rates to members. Membership also includes journals at generous discounts and gives access to courses, conferences, events, tours and regional and local activities. Full details are available from *The Secretary, The Historical Association, 59a Kennington Park Road, London SE11 4JH, telephone: 0171 735 3901.*

Contents

List of Illustrations

Introduction

The purposes of this pamphlet are twofold. First, it sets out how our thinking about the teaching of time has changed and developed since the early decades of this century. Much of what has gone before now serves to inform us in a number of ways. Chief amongst these is the fact that the assumptions of adults, both teachers and researchers, and the capabilities of children are profoundly influenced by the age in which they live. What is expected of children is similarly influenced. This seems self-evident, but it is something which is not always taken into account when research is being carried out, or when teaching activities are being planned. For instance, present day children's exposure, in literature and the media, to different versions of time in the past and future and to ideas of time travel, with all that entails, is very different from children's awareness of such phenomena in Piaget's day.[1] Recent research into children's understanding of time indicates that children possess much more awareness and ability than was thought when research of this kind began. These abilities are more apparent, however, when children are working with information and within a context which is familiar and appropriate to their level of intellectual development. We need, therefore, to take into account recent research and modern children's knowledge and understanding when considering the teaching of time.

The pamphlet's second purpose is to provide a range of examples and ideas drawn from current thinking and practice for implementing the teaching of time and chronology at Key Stages One and Two. It does not subscribe to the view of 'outline' history, or history seen as a mere succession of factual knowledge. Rather, it sets out to provide teachers with a range of strategies and techniques for fostering sound and fundamental temporal and historical concepts in the children they teach. Consideration of special educational needs in terms of children with learning difficulties and the very able is discussed where it is thought particularly appropriate. The requirements of the National Curriculum, along with children's developmental stages and social awareness, are factors which are given high priority in the sections which focus more directly on work in the classroom.

Guidance and suggestions for appropriate resources have been included to support classroom practice and further suggestions have been included in the appendices. These are, however, only a small sample of the vast range of materials available to support National Curriculum History, both at local and national levels. Teaching materials are changing each year at present and may continue to do so for some time until the revised curriculum becomes established.

What is meant by 'Time'?

Even before recorded history, people have held many different notions of time; what it is, how to measure it, how to represent it and how to record it. These problems have never been fully resolved or agreed upon. People have never achieved a fully rational explanation, so it is hardly surprising that both children and adults find it a difficult concept to understand and use. 'Time' cannot adequately be described as a single concept. It is a many-faceted notion, including clock time, calendar time, seasonal time, personal time, historical time, imaginary, or experienced time as opposed to 'real' time. It can be viewed as a mathematical, scientific or historical concept.

It can also be considered as a skill or set of skills. The ability to develop systems for comprehending and measuring time relies upon a range of important skills involving numeracy, literacy and memory. It can even be seen as a body of factual knowledge. The content of a history scheme or knowledge of the physical universe can both be seen as contributing factors which embody an understanding of either the passing of time or its measurement.

Early civilisations, such as Greece and Rome, often believed it to be, and represented it as, a deity, such as Kronos of the Ancient Greeks, who was believed to be the father of Zeus. Ancient Greek philosophers, such as Pherekydes, believed that chronos (time) was, indeed, the basic substance of the universe from which fire, water and air were derived. Many different civilisations throughout the world have represented time as a circle or wheel, possibly linking it strongly with the movements of the planets, or with seasonal time and the agricultural cycle. Some argue[2] that the analogue clock face is based on this archetypal notion of endless, cyclical time, dependent on the very movement of the universe in which we live.

Certain cultures, and particularly the Christian ideology which has permeated much of Western European culture, have represented time as linear. Possibly this view of time is based on the observation of the ageing process or permanent changes brought about by historical events. In Christianity, this image is linked with the idea that God's purpose continually moves forward towards its preordained goal, thus promoting the notion that the passing of time can be equated with progress. In Western physics, time has come to be seen as part of a mathematical framework. Attempts to reconcile the two notions of cyclical and linear time have produced the image of the helix. Interestingly, it was the recent discovery of D.N.A.[3], with its structure of the double helix, which has given such an impetus to research into genetics and the origins of all life forms.

Detailed systems for the measurement of time have evolved in different cultures. Many of these have been based on the notion of time as cyclical, resulting in detailed divisions and subdivisions of the circle or wheel. Some of the most sophisticated examples of such cyclical conceptions are found in the native civilisations of Central and South America, such as that of the Aztecs. Within each culture, it has been the task of the children to learn systems devised by their elders, communally understood systems often of considerable complexity. For example, the inhabitants of Madagascar use of typical events of their daily routine as their time markers, such as 'in the frying of a locust'.[4] Possibly these forms of time measurement are easier for children to understand than the more abstract notions formalised into complex systems in many cultures.

Apart from all these differing communal notions of time, there is also that dimension of time which is difficult to convey to others, our own personal experience of the passing of time and the perceived duration of an event. Described by Piaget[5] as 'psychological' or 'local', children have their own experience and understanding of this form of time, probably well before they begin to learn the conventions of their own particular culture.

The concept of 'historical' time is also very complex and is commonly expressed in the form of chronology. This is defined by the Shorter Oxford English Dictionary as 'The science of computing time or periods of time, and of assigning events to their true dates.' To be able to place events accurately in the past, children need to learn how to measure time accurately and also what is characteristic of each age. They find this conventional chronology difficult to understand and learn, particularly the chronology of time over a long period, covering many different epochs in history as well as relating these to appropriate dates. Christian children learn about B.C. and A.D., while children from other cultures have to be familiar with other counting systems, such as the Islamic Anno Hegira (A.H.), which measures time from an event in the life of Muhammad. For example, 1995 A.D. is the same year as 1373 A.H. Common Era (C.E.) is now beginning to be used to overcome some of these difficulties.

However, the learning which eventually culminates in an understanding of chronology begins early in life and takes different forms. Both children and adults understand and represent their notion of historical time in many ways, such as lines, circles, tunnels, spirals, 'targets', or three dimensional cones. When asked to illustrate their concept of time, adults often refer to their own background knowledge as a point of reference, so that a geologist will draw a long line, with 'man' represented as a very tiny dot at the end. An historian, on the other hand, may frequently draw a line illustrating time since recorded history began with the stereotyped images of different historical periods, such as the Parthenon, a Roman soldier and so on. A person thinking more about the process of historical enquiry may draw an image representing the fragmentary nature of this work, such as a keyhole, through which only tiny glimpses of the past can be seen. What emerges from these discoveries about people's conceptions of time, however, is their diversity, a diversity which needs to be considered when thinking about methods for teaching and representing time to young children.

The Need for an Understanding of Time

In the case of Western cultures, children face the daunting task of learning 'clock' time, which has itself undergone a considerable change with the increased use of digital clocks. Far greater precision in the knowledge and use of time is now demanded of us than ever before. They also need to understand 'calendar' time in order to grasp the notions of months, seasons and years. These aspects of time have become, in modern society, an essential life skill, which all children need to master.

Children also need to grasp their own identity and place in time, in relation to general historical chronology. While there is some disagreement among historians about whether 'historical' or 'chronological' time underlies the learning of history, there are certain aspects of its study which require some basic understanding of time.

The National Curriculum for History at Key Stage One (KS1) and Key Stage Two (KS2)[6] specifically requires the acquisition of knowledge, skills and concepts which depend upon a significant degree of awareness about time. The Study Units cover long periods of time, some hundreds of years, and temporal skills and concepts appear throughout them. The volume of content to be taught in the study units of the National Curriculum for History has been significantly reduced in terms of its coverage of time spans. This has helped relieve the pressure on teachers. However, a significant degree of awareness and development of temporal concepts is still required at both key stages. Skills such as the ability to sequence are clearly rooted in an understanding of time and others, such as change or cause and effect, are reliant upon a prior understanding of temporal sequence.

There are also specific requirements regarding the development of awareness and skills in the understanding of time throughout the Level Descriptions (pages 15 to 17) and Key Elements, (pages 3 and 5) which are now considered important for planning and assessment purposes. Increasing knowledge of different periods in time, a developing skill in the use of language related to temporal concepts and considerable progress in understanding chronology are all required. Of particular note is the fact that, by level three, children are required to 'show their understanding of chronology' by their increasing awareness of different periods in time. By the end of KS2, pupils are expected, in the Key Elements, not only to understand and use the conventions of historical chronology, but should also be learning to locate their historical knowledge within it. These features are demanding for primary school children, and the teaching of time concepts will be an important issue to address in both the planning and assessment of primary history.

Time concepts and those related to them are significant in other curriculum areas, such as geography, religious studies and science, as well as history. Indeed, they are concepts which underpin much learning and the acquisition of general intellectual skills. They also entail the understanding and application of core skills such as literacy and numeracy.[7]

Time concepts, therefore, seem to be basic to children's general education and ability to cope with life. It is currently suggested that such concepts may be taught successfully in the primary school. This is a radical change from long-held views that time, particularly 'historical' time, is a concept not accessible to young children and best left till adolescence. The following sections examine research findings and literature on this subject, to ascertain how such a major shift in opinion has come about.

What is Known about Children's Understanding of Time?

a) Early Research: c.1920 – 1970

Much of the early research in both psychology and history has been profoundly influenced by the work of Jean Piaget.[8] He saw time as a difficult concept, rooted in the physical sciences, and one which could only be understood in relation to concepts of speed, movement, distance and space. Drawing close parallels with his general theory of development, Piaget found that children began to construct an understanding of time in fairly clearly defined stages. Moving from a state in which duration was merely experienced, through a phase in which they could order events and actions of personal relevance, they finally, with the onset of operational thought, acquired an understanding of conventional time concepts, involving measurement and eventually, chronology. Children thus tended to progress from a local, egocentric concept towards a grasp of objective time, which was not generally acquired until adolescence, about the age of fourteen or fifteen.

Much subsequent research replicated Piaget's work, and until recent decades has tended to accept and corroborate his findings. One such example is the work of Gustav Jahoda,[9] a social psychologist, who tended to emphasise the limitations imposed by children's lack of awareness in matters concerning time. He found that before the age of five children were not able to describe a recent event or to sequence pictures and that after the age of five, they were only capable of ordering events into 'earlier' and 'later', and that success was dependent upon their familiarity with the content of the task.

His conclusions, based largely on previous research, suggested that children's understanding of clock and calendar time was similarly very limited. By the age of 5-6 they could understand the concept of yesterday, today and tomorrow; by age 7-8 they could grasp fully the concept 'weeks'; by 9-10 'months'; by 10-11 'seasons'; and not until early adolescence, the concept of last year, this year, and next year. Other research into concepts important in the study of history as it was taught in the first half of the century appears to have been equally pessimistic in terms of what children might be expected to understand. Clearly, this had serious implications for any teaching or learning involving the use of time concepts.

According to Levstik,[10] most other studies until the early 1980s showed similar results. Moreover, what is noticeable is that many of the lines of enquiry in these studies related back to findings of the 1920s. Many studies also tended to accept and apply these initial findings along with the work of Piaget, thus leading those in the fields of education and history to conclude that history was at best a difficult subject for young children and at worst, quite unsuitable.

The important work of Vygotsky[11] indicated a pitfall which much early research failed to avoid, namely the tendency to equate children's verbal ability with conceptual understanding. As Vygotsky pointed out, lack of verbal skill does not necessarily imply lack of awareness of the concept. This makes the assessment of concept development in children a difficult process, and conclusions about the presence of concepts in children's minds very difficult to prove.

Conclusions based upon early research findings, therefore, no doubt more appropriate to teaching contexts at that time, appear to beg many questions and cannot necessarily be applied to present day approaches to primary teaching. We need to consider whether the kind of history which was being taught to children then is comparable to the content of our history curriculum now. Were teaching methods similar, and, indeed, were the children and their background experiences out of school similar to those of the present day? I imagine most answers to these questions would be 'no'. Recent findings have presented a more optimistic view of children's capabilities. They also suggest alternative approaches to the teaching of time and very different expectations of children's potential abilities.

b) Research since c.1970

Recent research has been marked by an intensification and diversification of approaches to the study of children's time concepts. In particular, there has been a far more critical stance taken towards the work of Piaget, with many of his research methods and findings coming into question, particularly their application to the primary teaching context and to the teaching of history.

Margaret Donaldson[12] and Peter Bryant[13] have questioned the structuring of Piaget's tests, arguing that children failed to perform well largely because they did not understand the purpose of their tasks or approached them from a different perspective. Jerome Bruner[14] has also long been a critic of Piaget, arguing that children's developing concepts are more influenced by social influences and language than by simple maturational stages. Foremost amongst the psychologists who have posed alternative analyses of the development of time concepts is Paul Fraisse,[15] who, after a significant amount of research with young children, has expressed much dissatisfaction with Piaget's work. He argues that it is important to overcome the traditional (1920s) distinction between subjective time and objective time, which is assumed in the work of Piaget, since even young children tend to make use of both aspects of time in estimating duration. He believes that both children and adults make use of the same information processing skills in their experiences of time, and that the differences between the capabilities of the child and the adult are not as fundamental as Piaget suggests. Children are simply less able to analyse the multiple data of experience and to establish the relations between changes. With increasing age, he argues, memory of previous events facilitates the processing of perceptual information. What is important, according to Fraisse, is understanding the different ways in which children adapt to time. These can vary according to their learning context and culture as well as their age and ability.

Friedman[16] has focused on the qualitative nature of children's understanding. He argues that much of the earlier research involving activities such as ordering cards actually tells us very little about the processes which underlie those performances. His research has identified three psychological models which he believes are used by young children in temporal ordering: the 'temporal string' or series of links between events; 'locative codes' or verbal lists; and 'spatial images' or diagrammatic representations. He concludes that flexible use of the third mode is a later development than the first two, becoming apparent in some children of five, thus accounting for the wide variations in abilities among children of this age. In general, however, he argues that certain developmental trends in the process of how children acquire time concepts have been suggested by several studies by psychologists.

Recent studies undertaken by historians have also been more optimistic about children's capabilities than was the case in earlier decades. A growing body of evidence has suggested the feasibility of teaching history in the early years of education. It is now becoming accepted that very young children can begin to acquire some appreciation and understanding of times past without waiting for more complex knowledge of time conventions to be learned.

John West[17] believes that:

> It is a fallacy to argue that children from the age of seven have no sense of time. The 'research' often vaguely referred to substantiate this view has been, since 1922, inconclusive and inconsistent.

He refers to the small samples and limited tests used by early researchers and I would add to this the questionable validity of studies carried out so long ago if applied to present day teaching and learning.

After extensive research in schools, West is convinced that children do develop a sense of time throughout their primary school years. In the course of a four year study,[18] West found that young children of seven and over could sequence artefacts and pictures accurately, often using historical knowledge acquired outside school. He argues that it is merely a 'numerical' sense of time which they find difficult. Instead, teachers should capitalise on what children can do, such as developing their sense of contemporaneity and their skill in 'time-placing', through the use of a classroom time line.

Much pioneering work with younger children has been carried out by Joan Blyth. Her early research findings suggested that carefully prepared schemes of work were needed for children of infant school age, since it was apparent that, even in their first year of formal schooling, they could learn general historical skills from activities such as stories, role-play and the handling and discussion of artefacts. She felt that during their second year in infant school, children could progress to the use of more specifically historical materials.

Her more recent work[19] indicates that young children at KS1 can perform similar sequencing tasks to those mentioned above, provided that they are not presented with too many items to process at once. They frequently, as was seen by John West, used their general historical knowledge to help them in solving problems, much of this knowledge clearly being derived from home. She also found that all age groups tested, from the ages of 5 to 9, could cope with ideas and details associated with the concepts of change and difference. Younger children's expression of thought was limited by lack of vocabulary. The work of Sylva and Lunt, referred to in Blyth, also suggests that while children of pre-school age notice number and past/present time, they cannot always express their understanding of these concepts.

Often, young children's understanding is influenced by their familiarity with the context and content of the tasks they are given. Research in the United States has arrived at similar conclusions. For instance, Linda Levstik[20] has looked at the connection between narrative and historical understanding. She argues that traditional investigations have failed to take sufficient account of the effects of context on understanding, especially the forms of discourse used. In retelling an appropriate (for age and ability) historical narrative, she found that seven, nine and eleven-year-olds all linked history to chronology, revealing a gradual refinement of their use of chronology to define history. She found that children as young as six or seven knew something about time and history. Her general conclusion indicates no fundamental change in the process of learning; development of historical understanding is more simply one of degree. In Britain, Hilary Cooper's research[21] into primary history suggests that there is a pattern in the development of concepts, which need to be taught, and are best learned through discussion. The belief that direct, structured teaching fosters the acquisition of time concepts and related language is reiterated in a number of recent research articles.[22] A more decisive approach towards the teaching of time, therefore, seems appropriate to the needs of present day children. Consideration of their general awareness of temporal concepts derived from outside school needs to be taken into account, as does the context in which new learning experiences take place. Children's abilities in language and numeracy, and their degree of ability in processing information are also factors in their capacity to develop further their temporal understanding.

How do Children Learn about Time in School?

Young children begin to understand time through the development of a number of skills and related concepts, and by acquiring knowledge through the use of different sources and first hand experiences. Much of this learning takes place in random ways, particularly at home. Young children have little grasp of historical chronology, yet even before the age of seven, certain precursors of this concept begin to develop, so that they begin to acquire some awareness of 'historical time'. Areas of experience in school, such as language and numeracy, are fundamental to the understanding of conventional ways of representing time. Increasing ability in sorting, sequencing and a developing 'sense of the past' also contribute to an emergent understanding of historical time.

Language plays a significant part in the development of historical understanding in the early stages. There are very few aspects of historical study which do not depend heavily upon language skills. Indeed, all areas of National Curriculum English[23] are used in the study of primary history, particularly reading, writing, speaking and listening. The History National Curriculum requires children at KS1 to use simple temporal words and phrases accurately, such as 'old', 'new', 'older', 'newer', 'before', 'after', and 'long ago'. Children are also expected to learn the days of the week, months of the year and how to refer to years. They will need to understand and use words like 'yesterday', 'tomorrow', 'next week' and 'last year'. The most effective way of ensuring that these words become part of children's active vocabulary is through speaking and listening. Talk and discussion, whether whole class, group or individual, provides a sound basis for further development of their use of temporal language. In the nursery and reception class, children learn through play, talking and listening to stories and it is through experiences like these that young children learn most about the use of temporal terms.

At KS2 the National Curriculum Orders refer to the need for children to acquire language relevant to an understanding of chronology, such as 'ancient', 'modern', 'century', and 'decade'. It includes the abbreviations B.C. and A.D. and terms that define different periods, such as 'Tudor' and 'Victorian'. Children are also required to know how to use terms describing more abstract historical concepts, such as 'invasion' and 'occupation'. It is important to remember, in addition to this, that it is necessary, particularly with younger junior children to provide opportunities for revision and practice in using historical terms taught at KS1, since these may well have been only partially understood at the time, or since forgotten. Many of the teaching strategies appropriate at KS1 will continue to contribute to the extension of children's language acquisition at KS2.

In the later primary years, the planned introduction and specific teaching of key historical terms through discussion contributes to the acquisition of temporal terms and concepts. John West argues that children often learn concepts through linguistic experience, as is recommended in the Bullock Report.[24] This experience is best acquired, he suggests, through peer group discussions in history, the teacher assuming the role of neutral instigator and facilitator. In his research, West found that peer group discussions in history produced the most favourable results with those children who had not previously demonstrated written or oral skill. Whether through peer group discussion or teacher intervention, the introduction of specific terminology needs to be planned as part of work in history.

Between seven and eleven, most children will progress from a grasp of personal chronology acquired in the early years towards understanding and developing skill in the use of conventional historical chronology. John West's view that children are able to develop a sense of time in primary school has become generally accepted and adopted in the National Curriculum guidelines. West distinguishes though between a 'sense of time' and chronology, arguing that children before the age of thirteen are unable to relate numbered years and intervals to historical sequences. Nevertheless, historical awareness broadens in the later primary years to include different historical periods as well as the personal and local past. Linguistic ability becomes more refined and extensive, allowing for the expression of more detailed and specific historical knowledge.

All these experiences combine to create a personal reconstruction of the past which is constantly extended and refined by subsequent experiences. Bruner's spiral curriculum[25] is as effective in the learning of history as in any other subject. The question for teachers of young children is how best to promote this ever-widening understanding of the past. The following sections examine experiences and activities which promote the growth of skills in language, sequencing and chronology.

a) Everyday experiences

Piaget has noted how the newly born infant quickly learns to look for its mother before feeding. This very early behaviour suggests the interaction of a number of rapidly developing infant abilities, particularly the recognition of the regular pattern of events and experiences. Such behaviour reveals that at the very outset, the child is exhibiting the beginnings of an ability to sequence, arising from its own needs. This continues to develop rapidly in infancy.

Children arriving in the nursery school and reception class have already begun to grasp the significance of the daily routine, and are beginning to make associations connecting the time of day with regular activities, such as meal-times, bed-times, and story-times. These understandings provide a useful basis for the early years teacher who can consolidate children's awareness of sequence through activities, such as talking and story-telling involving recall and prediction, the making of booklets and charts to record the day's events or pictograms of favourite activities in the week.

In the early years at school, children continue to learn about time from daily routines and regular annual events. Many are still learning about the conventions of clock and calendar time, but are able to recall and discuss events in the more distant past, such as 'last summer', 'last Christmas' or 'last year'. Some are beginning to grasp the significance of dates and know how to sequence events which are fairly close in time. Although before seven or eight, young children have little grasp of chronology, certain early concepts begin to develop which may be considered precursors of chronological understanding. There is an incipient awareness of past and present in the sense that children can recall a past event such as a birthday or the arrival of a new brother or sister.[20] They can also look forward to future events such as festivals which occur on a yearly basis. This cyclical awareness is one of the ways of internalising the passing of time which underlies a subsequent grasp of chronology.

The advent calendar and advent candles used in Christianity, for example, make children aware of the counting of days and measurement of time leading up to Christmas. Preparation for festivals such as Divali, Ramadan, Hanukkah and the Chinese new year perform the same function in other cultures. These events form important connections with children's own experiences and the wider world, and fulfil the role of useful time markers. There are many opportunities for cross-curricular work in school to enrich young children's developing awareness of chronological time. The cyclical nature of events such as festivals is reinforced in other ways, like the recurrence of the seasons and the regular patterns in the behaviour of plants and animals.

Young children hear much of the language associated with chronology, words such as years, centuries, and references to specific dates, and although not fully aware of their precise significance, children do become aware that these expressions are often used and occasionally make their own attempts at using them. By the age of eight or nine, children's increasing understanding of number and its application in measurement gives meaning to the words they hear. Daily writing of the day of the week or date, and the keeping of regular diaries are all small details, but ones which contribute to a sense of time passing through the application of the core subjects.

b) Oral history

A commonly used strategy for teaching about sequence and change is to use oral accounts provided by the children's families, visitors and by teachers themselves. Oral histories create great interest at a personal level. Their direct first-hand quality particularly appeals to children from seven to eleven, and the stimulus they generate will help familiarise the children with dates and terms to do with times in the past. Children can then be encouraged to place the events they have heard about, or recorded in writing or on tape, into an historical time frame using a sequence line or timeline and attach appropriate labels to them.

c) Using artefacts

Questioning and vocabulary essential to an understanding of time may be learned at KS1 in a simple activity involving the examination of an object such as an old glass bottle. How old is the bottle? Was it made long ago? Is it an old-fashioned bottle? All these words will be heard and, more importantly, they may be used by children in an appropriate and meaningful context, giving substance to the words, so that they may become part of their active vocabulary. With very young children, objects which they recognise are likely to be a useful starting point. This has been recognised and used extensively in published materials devised for the teaching of history at KS1.

Aesthetic experiences, such as handling, drawing and modelling old objects provide a firm foundation for future learning in history. The texture, weight and smell of artefacts will make a lasting impression upon young minds, and if this experience is linked to meaningful talk, linguistic experience very relevant to time will be acquired. Vocabulary used by young children is often surprisingly mature. Terms such as 'old-fashioned' are used even at a very early age, although this might become 'fashioned-old'. I often heard about 'fashioned-old' cars from my three-year-old. Another child at the age of four referred to 'the new days'. Although technically inaccurate, these phrases were always used in appropriate contexts, suggesting a real understanding of their meaning.

The 'feely bag' may be adapted for introducing historical items into the classroom, making use of other senses, but then leading to discussion of the objects as they are 'found'. Unfamiliar objects can provide an excellent stimulus if introduced as a 'mystery' object. In extensive conversations with small groups of six-year-olds about an old warming-pan, I found that there was no need for me to initiate any questioning, since this came spontaneously from the children as soon as I placed the warming-pan in front of them. They discussed at length what it might have been used for and concluded that because the handle was wooden, and the pan was metal, it must have been for holding something hot. It was a pan for cooking in a very large hot oven, hence the length of the handle!

Here the children were using their contextual knowledge of a time in the past, in this case Victorian, with which to associate the object. The weight, materials and texture of the warming pan, and the way in which it had been made, all became apparent to them during the time spent handling and talking about it. All these features contributed to their 'sense of time' in a different age. One child was particularly perceptive and knowledgeable in his questioning and answering, and when, at the end of the activity, I asked them how many years ago they thought the warming pan had been made, he answered, 'One hundred years.' That this was not simply a wild guess was confirmed when I suggested it could be even older. He replied, 'Perhaps it could be a hundred and fifty years then.' He was clearly beginning to link his impressions of an age with some internal concept of chronological time. This emergent sense of period may be extended by providing a variety of objects to handle and discuss which all come from the same period in time.

The comparison of two objects with the same use, but made in different ages, extends this notion of 'things from the past' into further thought-provoking discussion. Comparing an old marble-stoppered glass bottle, for instance, with a modern plastic one can stimulate discussion beyond how things have changed to encourage the children to consider why they have done so. Linking these ideas helps to make a simple observation into a more truly historical activity, and even if the children do make wild or inaccurate statements, they have, at least begun to engage in the type of thought process which is fundamental to work in history. Having aroused their interest, the teacher can then give them as much accurate information as is considered appropriate, explaining how and why the object was used and why it changed. The ordering of artefacts can provoke similar valuable talk.

Older children at KS2 make more extensive use of artefacts as sources for historical enquiry. The process of investigating objects for historical information gives rise to an enquiring approach and to the use of important language skills, such as the use of detailed questioning. It also stimulates language linked to thinking and problem-solving, language which is used increasingly in the later study of history. Informed questioning of an object can lead to 'common sense' conclusions which can then be verified through the use of other sources, thus providing a stimulus for further enquiry using a range of historical sources.

d) Using visual sources

Pictures provide equally stimulating sources for small group discussion. Children at KS1 can learn to 'picture read' and to look for clues to inform them and raise questions about past times. To talk about what is happening in a picture can promote thinking and speaking which leads to the development of temporal concepts. For example, a school photograph, taken in late Victorian times, stimulates questioning and comment about details such as the children's clothes, their teachers and their expressions. The children can begin to see that over time school life and behaviour has changed, and perhaps begin to think about why this is so.

Picture sequencing is an increasingly popular activity throughout the early years. My personal experience of picture sequencing with young children is that their abilities vary enormously. Using four stereotypical pictures taken from different historical periods, I asked a class of reception infants to put them into order. Most of the children did not really understand the purpose of the activity and had no grasp of the significance of the pictures. One four year old, however, quickly sorted out the pictures into the correct order and placed them in a line across his table in 'reading' order, from left to right. To check that he really understood what he had done, I asked him why he had put the pictures in that order and he gave a very logical answer for each one. Some children, therefore, appear to understand sequence at a very early age. Many reception and year one children are now successfully using pre-prepared sequencing pictures to develop this sense of time. Although some may produce a sequence in the reverse order, I would argue that if the logical progression of the sequence has been maintained, they are certainly demonstrating an awareness of the concept.

Comparing two pictures of a similar object or event from different periods can fascinate young children. They need to learn how to observe closely, to be aware of detail and how to extract information from a visual source. Discussion with an informed adult is essential in promoting these skills. Children with special needs who find it difficult to work alone or to write find this kind of activity very rewarding.

Children at KS2 use an increasing number of strategies to enable them to sort and sequence information in some logical way. The most frequently used strategy is that of searching for visual clues. In working on the topic of the Spanish Conquest of Mexico, I have observed seven and eight year olds reconstruct the order of events which occurred at the time, using a series of four pictures derived from an Aztec account. (figure 1) Children from eight or nine have been shown to be able to sequence seven or eight pictures.[27]

Figure 1. Examples of Aztec pictures from the Florentine Codex.

Picture sequencing activities are useful as assessment tasks, revealing much about the children's contextual knowledge of different times and their skill in assessing contemporaneity. They reveal the children's use of skills such as close observation to detail and the ability to make inferences from these details. The development of concepts such as similarity, difference and change can also be observed while children are in the process of sorting, comparing and sequencing sets of pictures. As an assessment activity it has the advantage of relying on behaviour which does not depend upon language for success, simply the child's grasp of the historical concept. Such materials can be used in assessing children with special needs, particularly those who find recording their work problematic.

e) Using story and literature

Questions involving historical understanding may be introduced in the context of looking at both fiction and non-fiction books, as well as in general discussion and 'sharing' times with the children. It is these familiar situations which, if used carefully, promote many skills fundamental to the learning of history in subsequent years. As Joan Tough[28] has pointed out, to pause and talk about the story assists children's understanding of it. Predicting what is going to happen next extends their awareness of the dimensions of past and future in stories, thus establishing one of the most important understandings which underlies all other concepts of time. It introduces them to the use of past and future tenses, aspects of language which can cause young children great difficulties. It also helps make children aware of the meaning of words such as 'before' and 'after' which can also cause confusion.

Everyday story-telling sessions also contribute to the growth of temporal understanding. Following a simple sequence of events and then retelling it helps to instil the need for a particular order in a story. Joan Blyth[29] has shown how children of four and five learn to appreciate the past in a somewhat romantic fashion through fairy tales and nursery rhymes. While listening to and retelling these, however, they are becoming familiar at a very early age with historical terms and phrases, such as 'long, long ago' and 'once upon a time', used in stories as cues to the listener that the story is set in the past.

The significance and value of story books for the young reader in developing early time concepts also merits consideration. Many simple infant picture and story books have recently been produced to support work on themes relevant to KS1 history.[30] Other story books such as *What's the Time, Mr Wolf* by Colin Hawkins and *The Very Hungry Caterpillar* by Eric Carle are already extensively used to teach clock and calendar time. Picture books, such as the many books about grannies, and stories like *Granpa* by John Burningham, might equally successfully be used to teach about ageing. The passing of time at different rates, comparing real time with imaginary time may be explored in books such as *Come Away from the Water, Shirley* by John Burningham. There are many beautiful picture books such as *Window* by Jeannie Baker, which explore environmental change over time and cyclical time. In fact, many of the different ways of conceiving time have been expressed in such story books.

Context and illustrations contribute to the child's sense of the past if the story is set or written in a different period. *Peepo* by Janet and Allan Ahlberg contains illustrations set either in or just after the Second World War, giving clues such as the gas mask on the mantelpiece. *My Naughty Little Sister* by Dorothy Edwards, published in 1952, contains excellent stories and illustrations characteristic of this period. The provision of literature, both for personal reading and as class stories read by the teacher will continue to provide a meaningful context for specific historical terminology. There is a wealth of historical fiction which can be selected for use as background for a particular period. For example, *Legions of the Eagle* by Henry Treece immediately introduces reference to the first Roman invasion of Britain; it begins, 'Part One - AD 43.' The writer introduces historical terms within a meaningful story context which is likely to be absorbed and remembered by children of this age. Similarly, *The Lantern Bearers* by Rosemary Sutcliff puts into context the end of the Roman occupation, making clear the chronology of the period from Roman to Anglo-Saxon, familiarising children with the use of these terms. There are also books which involve the device of time travel or time leaps. Stories such as *Tom's Midnight Garden* by Philippa Pearce use this device. They stimulate curiosity and interest while at the same time allowing the author to use the historical context of another age. Provided books such as these are accurate in historical detail, they can offer extensive background knowledge to support learning in history, providing a continuing thread throughout a history-led theme.

f) Using film

It is important not to neglect the influence of television and film on present day children. Many television and film dramas, and schools broadcasts are set in different times in the past and there is little doubt that these experiences contribute much to children's growing sense of past times. Children gradually build up detailed knowledge often derived from second-hand experiences such as these. For example, after watching a BBC schools broadcast on Elizabeth I[31], a six-year-old had noticed and remembered how you might address a man in those days, 'Oh, you would have to say 'Sire'.' It was clear that he had absorbed the manners and style of speech used in Tudor times from watching the broadcast. It is probably in this somewhat haphazard way both at home and school that children learn details relevant to different time periods. However, the understanding of how these periods relate and follow on from each other is not so easily acquired and needs specific teaching.

Between the ages of seven and eleven, television and film contribute to children's understanding of specific historical terminology, a factor which is highly significant in the establishment of an understanding of chronology and contemporaneity. While there are obvious problems with the use of materials from television and film, such as inaccuracies, anachronisms, the presentation of a particular perspective, or the imposition of a 'Hollywood' style upon events, there is still scope for carefully selected extracts of film, such as those taken from well researched films or broadcasts, where the accurate portrayal of historical context has been of paramount importance. For example, a brief extract from the feature film '1492' provides an accurate portrayal of the use of navigational instruments at that time, within an historical context. In addition, the vividness and impact of film is an asset worth exploiting for the interest level which it generates, especially for children with reading difficulties.

There is also a wealth of archive documentary film material available from various sources, of particular use for the study units 'Victorian Britain' and 'Britain since 1930'. Collections of original documentary film, dating back to the Victorian era, such as the *Moving Memories* series produced by the Manchester Metropolitan University,[32] can give a lasting and vivid impression of the past to young children and are valuable on account of their authenticity. Clips of film taken in a locality familiar to the children would especially have a very immediate appeal.

g) Problem-solving tasks

Specific activities may be devised to stimulate children's thinking and use of questions. The provision of a collection of objects, pictures and scraps of written information, with an open question to stimulate discussion can be a strong motivator and foster a questioning approach. For very young children a bag of babies' belongings, toys, or household items can stimulate questions. For older children at KS1 this approach can be developed, using, for example, a school bag belonging to a child of the same age as themselves or older, or a bag or basket belonging to a child from some time in the recent past. This activity is not difficult to devise as there are readily available children's objects from recent history and from Edwardian and late Victorian times. It combines the use of investigative language in making judgments about the age of the 'mystery person' from an examination of their belongings and decision-making about what kind and age of person would be likely to use such things.

Many children, especially from the age of nine, when their reading has become more fluent, enjoy referring to non-fiction or to real historical sources for their information. Problem-solving activities for the KS2 units, using a range of primary sources such as objects, maps, documents and also extracts from secondary sources such as newspapers and books can be set up as either class or group activities.

In the later primary years, children are increasingly able to use both text and number as well as visual clues to assist them in logical reconstructions of sequences of events. For instance, in work using written sources to establish the cause of a particular event, children aged between eight and ten were able to extract relevant information from newspaper articles and then order it chronologically so as to be able to understand the cause and effect of events which had occurred during and after the First World War.[33] It was only after dating the events and placing them in a time sequence that the children were then able to discuss the links between them and use their contextual knowledge of the period to assist them in working out what might have happened.

The discussion generated by this enquiry approach creates opportunities for the development of higher order language skills, such as language relevant to the thinking behind sequencing and chronology. This includes the construction of complex sentences and the use of connectives such as 'when', 'while', 'although' and 'if'. For example, children aged ten, discussing their First World War problem began to ask questions about the children in the story who were investigating the mystery, such as:

> If he died ten years after his wife and child had died, how long was it from when he died to when the children are investigating it?

The use of these extended sentences enables more complex thinking, encouraging the child to select and organise information and to relate sequences of events to cause and effect. Such language use is important in laying the foundations for future development in thought, speech and written work.

h) Using the locality

A 'detective' approach to history rarely fails to stir the imagination and interest of young children, and the locality is an excellent place in which their detective skills may be put to good use. Julie Davies has explored the use of the locality in her article "Time Walk"[34] where she encourages young children of four to look carefully and begin to take note of details. The emphasis should be upon looking for similarities and differences between buildings, details on buildings, such as doors, windows and chimneys, and the materials which have been used. The teacher can then ask which buildings the children think are older than others and how they know. This approach will also eventually raise children's level of awareness and skill in observing their surroundings, providing a sound basis for local history work at KS2.

Photographs and drawings of streets and buildings in the locality are another well-known source for encouraging children to observe closely the contextual clues which indicate the period to which the pictures belong. Exploration of the reasons for changes in the use of buildings extends children's awareness of causation at KS2. Maps are meaningful to children at this age and are a useful source of sequencing material. Observation and sequencing of maps from different times in the past build on concepts of change and causation.

The number of places worthy of a visit is almost limitless. Churches are found in any locality and most church precincts are in themselves historical sites. The church building itself, where styles of building, furnishings and artefacts can date back to times in the very distant past, create in the children a sense of times past which, although still somewhat unfocused, will help establish an idea of how the past may have been. Historic sites are frequently found in unusual or unexpected places, for instance, in the local park (ruins of a medieval priory, Dudley, West Midlands), or tucked away behind a modern industrial area (the oldest lending library in England, behind I.C.I. in an industrial suburb of Runcorn, Cheshire). Even when your school is part of a modern housing development, it is often possible to find fairly nearby some houses dating from the 1930s or some Victorian terraces. One housing estate in Manchester was built by prisoners of war during the 1940s. The locality does not need to be steeped in a long and varied history for it to hold teaching potential for young children. After all, for them, the recent past is history.

Many museums are now devising new and varied ways of creating a sense of period by reconstructing the past. These museums attempt to 'bring history to life' by recreating entire streets (Larkhill Place, Salford) or parts of towns and villages (Black Country Museum, Dudley; Jorvik, York). There are also working museums, such as the Gladstone Pottery Museum, Stoke-on Trent, and Styal Mill, Cheshire. Children experience the sights, sounds and smells of a bygone age, perhaps not in a fully authentic way, but in sufficient detail to provide them with some contextual knowledge with which to associate Victorian, or Viking times. John West, in his book *Classroom Museum*,[35] provides an extensive list of museums, organised under topic headings.

One strength of work on local history is its value in establishing a first hand context for terms such as 'Victorian terrace' or 'Tudor house'. If children have had the experience of studying real examples of places like these in the locality or at historic sites and museums, they will have some contextual knowledge with which to link other examples of features characteristic of Victorian or Tudor times. Local studies can thus give real and accurate meaning to the words and assist the process of establishing a sense of contemporaneity within historical periods.

i) Using role play and simulations

Some museums, such as the Heritage Centre in Macclesfield with its operational 'Sunday School' classes, provide opportunities for role play activities. While there are obvious dangers that children may be frightened or confused by these interactive experiences, the advantages must outweigh such considerations. Simulated play areas can provide much enjoyment and first hand appreciation of certain features of life in past times. Many accounts of this type of activity are to be found in books and journals on the teaching of history.[36]

By the age of eight or nine, the National Curriculum requires children to begin to use abstract terms such as 'civilisation', 'invasion', and 'slavery'. Classroom simulations and role play activities are ways of giving substance to terms which are often obscure to primary children. For example, when studying Ancient Greece, a class could explore the meaning of the word democracy by thinking of different ways of making decisions, including the notion of everyone voting. They could then set up a simulation of a vote in Ancient

Greek times, when women and slaves were excluded. Their awareness of the meaning of 'democracy' would thus be considerably extended. By putting themselves in the same situation as people in the past, children can absorb more fully the meanings of difficult conceptual terms which are of central importance in any further study of history.

j) Learning about Time Through Mathematics

Chronological understanding is partly bound up with the ability to sequence, to measure time and to place events in time according to conventional terminology. It also requires the establishment of a sense of the past. In young children this is a generalised awareness of the past in the sense of 'long ago' or 'a very long time ago'. With increasing maturity, certain children in the infant school, but mostly children moving up the junior age range, will begin to acquire a sense of period, upon which an understanding of historical chronology partly rests. Primary teachers therefore need to provide opportunities for children to organise and measure time and to begin to establish this sense of period.

i) Numeracy

There are many opportunities for children from four to seven to link their early grasp of cardinal and ordinal numbers with the sequencing of events, objects or pictures. By KS2, children's understanding of number embraces larger calculations involving hundreds and thousands. This increasing awareness of number helps them in their attempts to understand the significance of dates and spans of time. In the later years of KS2, they can be shown how to calculate ages, or the time which has elapsed between events through the use of simple subtraction. Their increasing understanding of place value may also help them in placing events in chronological order, or in placing an event on a dated timeline. They also need an understanding of ordinal numbers, negative numbers needed to grasp the significance of 'B.C.', and a higher level of knowledge of the language of number, such as 'decade', 'century' and the usage and meaning of terms such as 'the sixties' and 'nineteenth century'.

Mathematical work on pattern and sequence in number may also assist them in understanding the pattern in the increasing size of dates as they progress through time. An association of the characteristic features of different ages with specific numbers may, at this stage help children to acquire some sense of chronology and to understand the need, in history, to place periods and events as precisely as possible within a time frame.

Many nine, ten and eleven year olds will have acquired sufficient grasp of number and graphicacy to enable them to use and begin to construct their own timelines, incorporating some key dates. As John West has found, they can be taught how to calculate ages and time spans by using dates given on a timeline. Practice in activities like this will also improve their mathematical skills.

ii) Graphicacy

Skills involved in the reading and construction of charts and timelines are rooted in mathematics. Diagrams and matrices are often similar to those used in mathematics, as is the representation of long periods of time through the use of scale. In particular the calculations involved in the drawing up of time charts use many mathematical skills, for instance calculating how many years may be shown on paper of a particular size, how different features need to be related to dates and how the organisation of columns, rows and boxes influences the meaning of the chart. All of these considerations are difficult for children of eight or nine and need teacher support and advice. They would adequately 'challenge' the able child of ten or eleven, working individually or in groups.

k) Other Cross Curricular Links

Drama, art, music, science and technology can all contribute to a growing sense of the past. Young children would not be expected to think consciously about the exact chronological placing of know–ledge learned from such experiences as looking at paintings or listening to music; this would probably be quite inappropriate before the age of seven or eight. What is important is the experience itself and the enjoyment and appreciation of something from the past, which will hopefully remain for them to build upon in later years. At KS2 this growing awareness of the age in which these works of art were created will contribute to children's developing sense of time and ability to place characteristic features within their own time frame.

How do children begin to make sense of these random and often confusing encounters with history in such different forms? One method is for the teacher consciously to show how the past can be organised and ordered through the use of sequence and timelines, which may take any form and use models, artefacts, pictures or written information. Chapter five examines this aspect of learning about time in more detail.

Using Timelines in National Curriculum History

a) The value of the timeline

The content required by the National Curriculum for History at both Key Stages is broad-ranging and covers periods remote both in time and place. Schools may choose to study these in a chronological sequence or they may decide to use the teaching strengths of their staff and allow them to select National Curriculum themes, thus resulting in a non-chronological order in the teaching of the history units. Whatever method is chosen, but more so in the case of the non-chronological study of units, there is a real need for some visual representation of the time periods being studied. There is also the need for a unifying, chronological overview of all the periods being taught. The timeline has been widely adopted as the most appropriate type of chart for meeting these needs.

Helen Madeley, author of an early Historical Association Pamphlet on *Time Charts*[37] has been vindicated, it seems, in her prophesy that the timeline '...will probably be the chart of the future.' As she points out, its strengths are that it is cheap to make and simple to use. It is a very flexible tool since it can be used for all periods and all kinds of developments, world or family history. It is also so versatile that it can be adapted for use on either the small or large scale, to be used within a book or for display in a large hall. When completed, the timeline can become an attractive display item, serving as an end product in the collection of material on a theme.

Timelines can take many forms: 'washing lines'; three-dimensional lines; circular, for showing cyclical patterns eg. days, seasons, or festivals (figure2); vertical or horizontal two-dimensional friezes; 'scroll' or rolled charts, as described by Helen Madeley (figure3).

Figure 2. Circular booklet

Figure 3. Rolled chart or scroll timeline

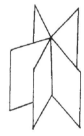

b) The uses of the timeline

The timeline is useful for quick reference, a visual aid for the teacher as well as for the children, and can be displayed for this purpose. Charts intended for use in this way, however, will need to be very clear and uncluttered. A timeline created by the teacher can serve as an aid in planning and organising a history-led theme. Deciding what to include and how much space to allocate to particular episodes can help clarify in the teacher's mind the key teaching points.

At the beginning of a topic, an introductory chart giving a brief overview of the whole period is invaluable. These can either be purchased[38] or home made. Such charts are, however, only intended for showing major landmarks and a few key dates within the period of study. If kept simple, they can be useful in introducing children of seven or eight to the notion of dates and chronology.

More detailed charts can illustrate overlaps, contemporary periods or events and spans of time. Visual representation of relative lengths of time such as reigns is often quick and memorable and useful for making comparisons. A timeline of sources affords the opportunity to see at a glance how much is known about different periods in time, by revealing our current state of knowledge.

To be fully understood, the timeline needs to become an integral part of work on an historical theme. In order to involve the children in reading the chart and finding out how it works, questions need to be asked either verbally with the whole class, or on work cards or sheets, with the children working in pairs to find the answers. They can then discuss and check their findings.

The timeline is a means of utilising many of the children's emerging abilities in language, mathematics, sequencing and their developing 'sense of time'. A flexible line is useful in stimulating discussion and in allowing the children to create their own versions of the past. They can discuss choices of material for the line and the placing of items on it, moving them around as they change their minds or find new information. Decisions about organisation, scale and measurement will involve the application of mathematical concepts and skills. The timeline can also serve as a stimulus for the natural 'collecting' impulse, requiring them to sort and sequence their findings logically and according to their knowledge of past times.

c) Time-related tasks and sequence lines for KS1

Very young children will begin to understand the idea of temporal sequence and order by first seeing and creating arrangements of three dimensional objects according to which is new, old and oldest. By the end of the key stage, very able children might begin using a sequence line which includes a few dates. In order to achieve progression, teachers might:

- Provide meaningful objects for very young children, such as toys, clothes, or household items for children to sequence, starting with the oldest.

- Select more objects for sequencing, corresponding with the increasing age and ability of the children. Sequences made by young children may be logical, but not necessarily arranged in the way the teacher would expect, such as a straight line or in reading order. Children may organise objects in an apparently random way at first glance but may attach some significance to it themselves, as is often the case with children's early drawing.

- Question and discuss the reasons for their sequencing in order to see what it actually means to them. This will also enable the teacher to see whether or not they have understood the purpose of the task and allow the provision of individual support and clarification where needed.

Figure 4. 'Growing up' book

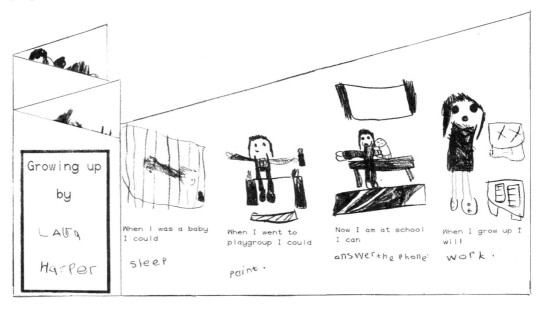

- Gradually begin introducing objects from the past to sort or compare with their present day counterparts. Historical objects such as those used by their parents or grandparents provide meaning to the activity for young children.

- Show children of six or seven how to create their own books. Folding booklets, similar to an early timeline, are useful for recording memorable events of the day or week. These could be designed to fold up concertina-like, or folded and joined to form a circular booklet, to represent the continuous and cyclical nature of time.

- Make 'growing up' booklets showing the child's growth as the story unfolds. (figure4)

- Make circular mobiles of the months or seasons.

- Use flexible lines, such as a 'washing line' upon which cards can be placed and moved around. A simple version of this line is frequently used in infant classrooms, usually consisting of a single line stretching across the room containing cards with words or pictures related to the class's current theme. 'Washing lines' showing the days of the week in reception or year one classes can be altered in year two to show the order in which a group of famous people were born. The children could be prompted to think about the reasons behind the placing of new people on the line. It is a particularly useful device for representing simply the idea of 'past', 'present' and 'future', to which the children can add new information and change the positions of events from the future or present into the past as time moves on.

- Make a simple sequence line in the form of a more permanent folding book. This could include pictures of any topic of current interest, or it could be a collection of pictures characterising different periods in history. There are problems in the selection of such a set of pictures. Children need to begin with a simple collection of images. However, these may represent only one view of history or reflect one particular set of assumptions about the past. More than one set of images should be presented in order to avoid this problem arising.

- Begin to create simple sequence lines for display. Children's own pictures, drawings and models can be arranged sequentially according to chronology. While dates may mean little as yet, there is no harm in representing the passing of time in an accurate order and using the assembled pictures as reference points when talking to children.

- Illustrate everyday life in their own families, then link it with everyday life in a period in the past using a simple sequence line. Contemporaneity should be illustrated through aspects of life, such as dress, transport, or buildings, grouped together for each period.

- Make a 'time box'. Discuss what things they might put in it to interest future historians.

- Encourage the children to use the sequence line. They could either collect, make, or be provided with further pictures, which they would need to place correctly, matching the detail of their illustration with the appropriate period on their line. This activity is best done on a large table or on the floor to allow children to arrange their pictures for the teacher to check before actually sticking them on. Alternatively, children can be asked to re-order a set of pictures incorrectly placed on the line, and to explain why they are moving the pictures. In this activity children will learn some of the characteristic features of periods in the past and will also begin to establish the concept of contemporaneity.

- Make variations of the sequence line, such as free-standing cards containing pictures or other information, which could be easily moved around.

- Make available for children to look at if they wish, a timeline showing the simple order of events or people and including a few key dates.

In dealing with times beyond living memory, the KS1 teacher has greater flexibility and choice of content than in any other area of the curriculum. Since the revision of the curriculum in 1995, by Sir Ron Dearing, more time is now available for teachers to focus upon their own or their children's interests and needs, in theory, at least. There might be opportunities for teachers to explore periods in history which are unlikely to be studied again in the primary years, such as Edwardian times, the Stuarts or the Norman Conquest and Middle Ages, all colourful, interesting periods which, in the past, have occasionally been taught in the primary school.

d) Timelines at KS2

- Provide a simple outline chart for the children to make their own timelines. An example of such a line is easily done as a whole class activity, giving, as a basis, common events as they happen in school, the children adding details personal to themselves after school time, such as going to birthday parties, shopping or going swimming. The whole class thus quickly learns how to make entries on their own chart.

The Northern Ireland Guidelines for timelines[39] gives suggestions for a progression of simple charts like these which gradually expand and become more complex as children gain greater familiarity with the process of making them. A similar list of charts for developing a sense of chronology is provided in the Final Order and Non-Statutory Guidance for Wales.[40] Also, *Teaching History at Key Stage One*,[41] produced by the National Curriculum Council suggests challenging timelines and sequencing tasks, which might be useful for younger or less experienced children at KS2.

- Build up class charts in the course of work with seven and eight year olds on a particular period. If a simple outline is provided by the teacher, containing two or three key dates, the class can then add information to it as the topic progresses. This could be in the form of objects, models, portraits, pictures, maps, drawings, written information or symbols. Collages and carefully made illustrations of people make very colourful and interesting display items.

- Use symbols, such as crossed swords for wars or crowns for new monarchs, as an incentive for enquiry work. Place symbols like these on the new line, giving the children the task of researching to find what event the symbols represent.

- Use this type of 'working' timeline as a culminating piece of display work, drawing together the key elements of the term's work in history.

- Plan a general timeline for keeping in the centre or back of children's books, moving with the children to each new class and added to as each new historical period is studied. This gives them an overview of the whole span of history they have studied and provides a useful record for the school and for parents.

- Alternatively, have each child keep a folding, concertina timeline inside stiff board covers, to stand the passing of time. It needs to be made of strong paper and the folds strengthened with book-binding tape. This could well become a treasured possession long after leaving primary school, in much the same way as 'best' books, hand made and beautifully decorated for preserving best pieces of work, are made in many schools. Many varied ideas for creating books which could be used for work on time are suggested in the work of Paul Johnson.[42] He has used 'folding' and 'opening door' techniques to good effect and these ideas could easily be adapted for historical purposes.

- Use timelines to show the coincidence of events or periods. If, for example, a comparison of events in another part of the world needs to be made with British history, then the two histories can run in a parallel fashion, with British history on one side of the line and the comparative history on the other. Children can then see at a glance the similarities and differences between the two histories, as well as which events were happening contemporaneously. Lines such as these are also helpful for the teacher, in order to relate periods of time in other parts of the world with more familiar aspects of the history of Britain. This is particularly useful in the case of the pre-Columbian civilisations, which are frequently referred to as 'Ancient', and consequently equated, in terms of chronology, with the Ancient Egyptians or Greeks, when in fact cultures such as the Aztecs and Incas are contemporary with the early Tudors in Britain. Publishers are now becoming aware of the value of this type of information and there is, at present, one chart available which shows the synchronism between Tudor England and Benin. (figure5)

- Use information technology as a quick way of creating timelines once the concept has been grasped. One computer version of a timeline has as its basis British history, but allows any other histories to be compared.[43] An example program is provided, showing British history and world history on either side of the horizontal line. The program is 'content free' however, which means that its real purpose is for users to enter their own information. So world history could be replaced with the history of a country,

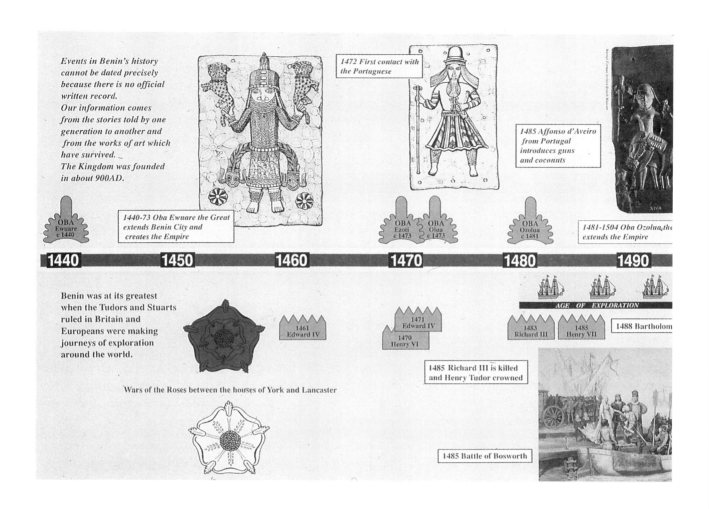

Events in Benin's history cannot be dated precisely because there is no official written record.
Our information comes from the stories told by one generation to another and from the works of art which have survived.
The Kingdom was founded in about 900AD.

1472 First contact with the Portuguese

1485 Affonso d'Aveiro from Portugal introduces guns and coconuts

OBA Ewuare c 1440

1440-73 Oba Ewuare the Great extends Benin City and creates the Empire

OBA Ezoti c 1473

OBA Olua c 1473

OBA Ozolua c 1481

1481-1504 Oba Ozolua the extends the Empire

1440   1450   1460   1470   1480   1490

Benin was at its greatest when the Tudors and Stuarts ruled in Britain and Europeans were making journeys of exploration around the world.

1461 Edward IV

1471 Edward IV

1470 Henry VI

AGE OF EXPLORATION

1483 Richard III

1485 Henry VII

1488 Bartholom

Wars of the Roses between the houses of York and Lancaster

1485 Richard III is killed and Henry Tudor crowned

1485 Battle of Bosworth

Above, Extract from the Kingdom of Benin Timeline (fig.5).
Below, Extract from Time Lines (fig.6).

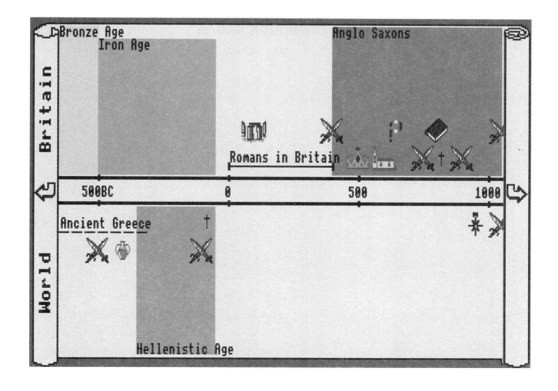

or with the local history of the user's area. It would be equally useful for comparing a family history with either local or British history. (figure6)

- Encourage very able children to explore contemporary periods or events and illustrate them in parallel lines one above the other. Many books are now available on this topic, one of which is most useful as a teachers' resource for a study of the Ancient civilisations. *Timelines of the Ancient World: a Visual Chronology from the Origins of Life to AD 1500* by Chris Scarre,[44] includes numerous photographs of original sources, useful for reference and as a source of details for inclusion on a more modest chart for the classroom.

- Make simple charts to show when key festivals and events in different religions occur throughout the year, using a synchronous line like that mentioned above. Cross-curricular work, combining both history and religious studies, for example, enriches the study of both subjects and also provides opportunities for the development of children's chronological awareness of other cultures and religions. This activity also serves as a reminder to teachers of the various religious festivals which they may wish to take into account when planning. A detailed example of such a chart is available from SHAP.[45] This might serve as a resource from which the teacher and class could create their own version appropriate to their particular context.

- Record changes in the local community on timelines about the school or locality. The timeline should allow children to compare local history with events and changes at a national level.

- Create timelines about historic sites or places of interest. My year three class created one such timeline on the theme of Chester Cathedral, which proved to be an excellent source for the study of change from Saxon to modern times. It is an activity which can be easily replicated in local areas, with a church, castle or any historic site with a reasonably long history.

- Encourage able children to make individual timelines to record work on their own particular interests or projects. Children learn a great deal about the problems of drawing diagrams and constructing charts, such as the need to be linguistically accurate, concise and clear. They also begin to recognise the mathematical considerations involved in creating a line to encompass a long period of time, thus bringing into

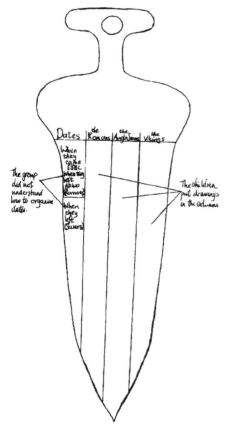

Figure 7. A timeline produced by year 4 children at Stockton Heath Primary School.

use their knowledge of scale and representation, accuracy in measuring and careful calculation so as to have an accurate record of their findings. Making timelines on individual themes to record work done earlier by the class can become a very useful activity for assessing children's developing understanding of chronology. Children whom I asked to make their own charts began to understand the problems involved and displayed a considerable grasp of the order in which developments took place. They designed very original visually attractive charts and it was interesting to note that they were far more inclined to draw a timeline which had as an outline, an object or picture, rather than the typical, more abstract timeline. (figure 7)

- Make different types of time chart, such as the checkerboard chart, referred to by Helen Madeley. This appeals very much to the desire to collect scraps of information, so characteristic of children of this age. The chart is like a hundred square, in which each line of ten squares represents a decade. The children's task is then to find an item of information to put in each square. Filling such a chart could be used as a 'spare time' activity in a course of work on the nineteenth century/Victorians, either as an individual, group, or whole class collaborative activity.

- Try to create a space for a whole school timeline. In some schools, the process of giving an overview of the whole of the school's history curriculum at KS2 is catered for in the form of a very large timeline housed round the walls of the school hall. Then, as any child or class completes a good piece of work, such as a very careful piece of art work, it can be added to the school timeline. In one school which has this as a regular feature of its work in history, the head teacher takes the opportunity to refer to the timeline and make use of it on occasion in assemblies, thus ensuring that every child is aware of its purpose.

Fig. 8: A suggested timeline for seven-year olds: the Romans

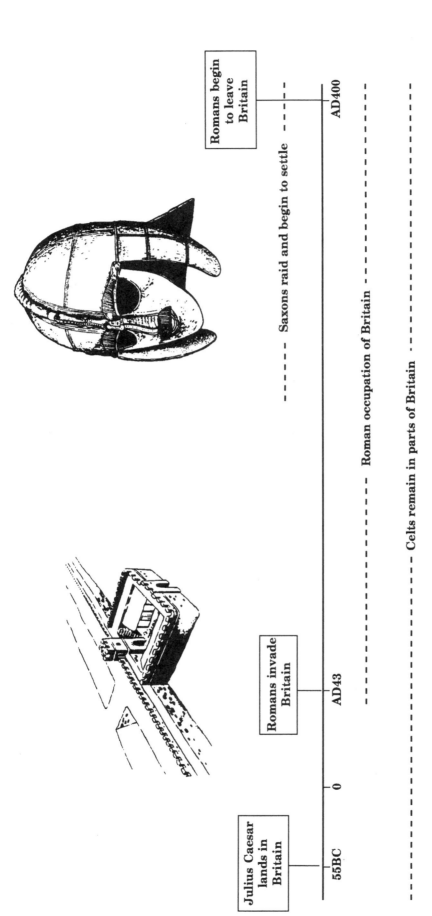

Julius Caesar lands in Britain		Romans invade Britain		Romans begin to leave Britain
55BC	0	AD43		AD400

- - - - - Saxons raid and begin to settle - - - - -

- - - - - Roman occupation of Britain - - - - -

- - - - - Celts remain in parts of Britain - - - - -

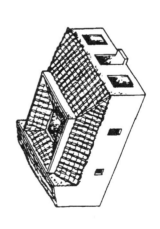

e) Examples of Timelines for the study units at KS2

Progression is achieved at KS2 by developing children's understanding from the sequence line with very few dates for Year 3 into a conventional, dated timeline for Year 6. Whichever unit is being studied by children of seven or eight it is best for them to begin by using a simple sequence line, showing the order in which events took place. The grouping of five or six contemporaneous items and events will at first be enough for the young junior child of seven or eight. However, once the order has been grasped, they might then be ready to add a few important dates. (figure8)

Children of eight or nine will be able to grasp the significance of key dates which will need to be introduced gradually. By the age of ten or eleven, children are expected to be able to use terminology, dates and the conventions for recording the passing of time. These features, therefore, may usefully be introduced on the timeline, which will become more detailed, informative and precise by the end of KS2, similar in appearance to a conventional timeline, although more limited in terms of content or selection of information.

Numerous types of questions can be based on the timelines, from simple information retrieval and calculations of duration for younger children, to open questions requiring more thought and consideration of causation for ten and eleven year olds. An activity which many children find demanding is asking them to devise their own questions for their friends to answer.

Each Study Unit presents its own particular demands and problems dependent upon the range and type of content it covers. I have included timelines from different periods here to illustrate ways of addressing specific problems in the case of units such as Victorian Britain, Ancient Egypt and the Aztecs. Consequently, each timeline varies slightly in its scale, structure and composition. Timelines may be constructed or read in any direction, but the author's preference is for vertical lines to be read from top to bottom, and for horizontal ones to be read from left to right. These examples have been designed for reading in this way. A school may decide upon the use of one type of timeline only, or upon the use of a variety of timelines, focusing upon the principles behind their construction. Whichever approach is considered best for a particular school, it is suggested that it is adopted and used throughout the school.

The following timelines are intended for teachers, to provide initially an overview of some of the main features of the study units, and secondly, to provide a basis for further development by either teachers or pupils. The teacher may wish to select certain information relevant to a theme to create a simplified version of a timeline for a class of younger pupils, or to use it as a basis for building up a more complex picture with more able children at KS2. The timelines may also be used by older or more able children to help them plan their own timelines or associated work.

Fig. 9: Romans, Anglo Saxons and Vikings in Britain
Study Unit 1

55BC — Roman fleet off coast Julius Caesar

AD563 — St. Columba preaching Christianity

0 —

AD597 — St. Augustine preaching Christianity

AD600 — Britain divided into seven main Anglo-Saxon kingdoms

AD43 — Roman occupation

AD622 — Sutton Hoo ship burial of King Redwald

AD62 — Boudicca's revolt

AD635 — Lindisfarne monastery founded

AD657 — Abbey at Whitby founded by Hilda

AD128 — Hadrian's Wall completed

AD731 — Bede completes his History

AD735 — Death of Bede

AD758 — King Offa (758-796)

AD793 — Vikings attack Lindisfarne

ROMANS
CELTS
SAXONS
CELTS

AD250 — Saxon pirate raids begin

AD834 — First Viking raids in southern England

AD849 — Vikings begin to make permanent settlements Viking kingdom of Jorvik

AD300 — First coastal forts to prevent Saxons landing

AD871 — King Alfred (871-901); Anglo-Saxon Chronicle begun

AD313 — Christianity accepted by Rome

AD878 — Guthrum the Dane defeated by Alfred

VIKINGS

AD350 — Hadrian's Wall rebuilt after Celtic and Saxon raids

SAXONS

AD400 — Roman troops begin to leave

AD991 — Battle of Maldon: Saxons vs. Vikings

AD410 — Roman troops no longer supported

AD1016 — Danish raids begin again; Danegeld; King Canute; peace between English and Danes

AD432 — St Patrick preaching Christianity in Ireland

AD1066 — Norman Conquest: William I

Study Unit 1: Romans, Anglo-Saxons and Vikings in Britain

The major consideration when planning to teach about time in relation to this study unit is the very long period which the unit covers. It includes the years from 55 BC to the early eleventh century, and although only one of these societies needs to be studied in depth, there is a need for children to become aware of the sequence of events and relative duration of successive civilisations throughout the whole period. Joan Blyth[46] points out that 'Teachers should constantly make comparison and contrast between the three different invaders and try to see how they link with each other' (p 31). A general timeline of the entire period is, therefore, essential for children to grasp the changes which took place over this long period of time and to begin to understand the B.C., A.D. divide. A supplementary line would need to be produced for the particular period, Romans, Saxons or Vikings to be studied in depth.

What is particularly interesting about this entire period is the great extent of 'overlap' between the three civilisations. Saxon invasions took place during Roman times, just as Viking invasions were common during the Saxon period. For long periods of time two societies lived contemporaneously. A brief glance at a timeline also shows that an equally long era was spanned by the Anglo-Saxons as, for instance, by the Romans. The timeline is a very quick and effective way of illustrating these points to young children and also provides a focus for discussion and questioning on issues such as these. (figure 9)

FIG.10: LIFE IN TUDOR TIMES

Study Unit 2

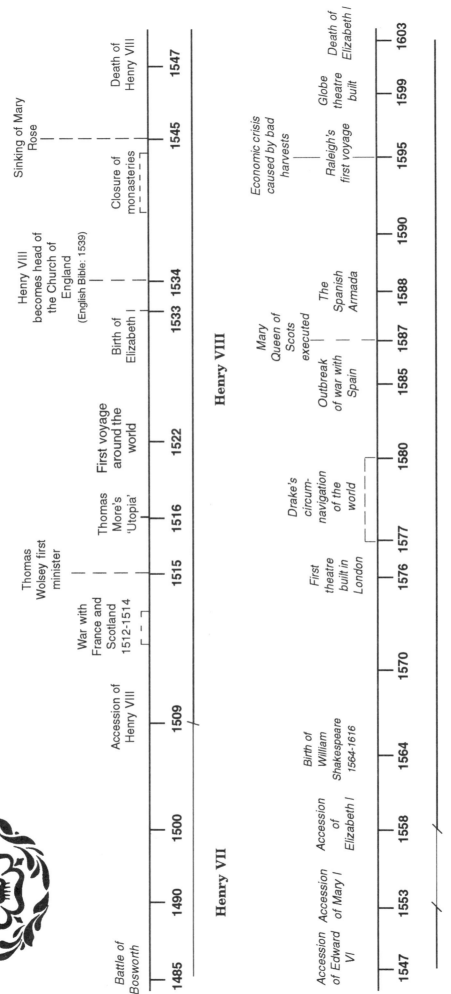

Henry VII

Henry VIII

Elizabeth I

Edward VI **Mary I**

Battle of Bosworth — 1485

1490

1500

Accession of Henry VIII — 1509

War with France and Scotland 1512-1514

Thomas Wolsey first minister — 1515

Thomas More's 'Utopia' — 1516

First voyage around the world — 1522

Birth of Elizabeth I — 1533

Henry VIII becomes head of the Church of England (English Bible: 1539) — 1534

Closure of monasteries

Sinking of Mary Rose — 1545

Death of Henry VIII — 1547

Accession of Edward VI — 1547

Accession of Mary I — 1553

Accession of Elizabeth I — 1558

Birth of William Shakespeare 1564-1616 — 1564

1570

First theatre built in London — 1576

Drake's circumnavigation of the world 1577 — 1580

Outbreak of war with Spain — 1585

Mary Queen of Scots executed — 1587

The Spanish Armada — 1588

1590

Economic crisis caused by bad harvests

Raleigh's first voyage — 1595

Globe theatre built — 1599

Death of Elizabeth I — 1603

Study Unit 2: Life in Tudor Times

The emphasis in this period of history is often upon the dynastic succession, dominated by Henry VIII and then Elizabeth I, the two monarchs with the longest reigns, as is easily illustrated on a timeline. However, it is important to indicate that there were many significant personalities in Tudor times as well as the monarchs, such as Shakespeare, the explorers, Drake and Raleigh, and those with whom the monarchs had to deal, such as Mary Queen of Scots, Thomas Wolsey and Thomas More. There is also a wealth of lesser known, more ordinary Tudor personalities who could be suitable subjects for study.[46]

Major events are also easily depicted on a timeline, although there is still a need for ruthless selection on the grounds of what might be meaningful to young children. As Joan Blyth rightly points out the 'break with Rome' is a difficult concept and one which occurred over a long period of time, but it is still possible to indicate the period in which many of the monasteries were closed. (figure 10)

FIG 11: VICTORIAN BRITAIN

Study Unit 3a

POLITICAL	ECONOMIC	SOCIAL	CULTURAL
1837 Victoria becomes Queen		1838 First pinhole camera 1839 Education Act	1838 Oliver Twist published
1840 Victoria marries Prince Albert	1841 Great Western Railway completed 1843 Great Britain launched	1842 Mines Act 1844 Rochdale Pioneers Co-operative Society 1846 Irish potato famine 1847 10 hours Factory Act	
	1846 Repeal of the Corn Laws	1848 Cholera epidemic: Public Health Act	1848 Pre-Raphaelite Brotherhood formed
1854 to 1856 Crimean War	1851 Great Exhibition	1854 Cholera epidemic 1855 Florence Nightingale begins reforms	
			1859 Darwin's theory of evolution
1861 Death of Prince Albert	1863 First London underground railway	1860 Louis Pasteur discovers microbes	1863 Football Association formed
1867 Second Reform Act	1867 Typewriter invented	1867 Workshop Act	1865 Alice's Adventures in Wonderland published
1871 Secret Ballot	1869 Suez Canal opened	1870 Elementary Education Act	
		1875 Public Health Act	
	1876 Bell's telephone		
1877 Victoria given title "Empress of India"			
	1879 Edison's electric light bulb	1881 Compulsory education	
1884 Third Reform Act	1884 Daimler invents petrol engine		
1887 Victoria's Golden Jubilee	1886 Benz makes first motor car		
	1888 Pneumatic tyre invented by Dunlop	1891 Free education	
		1894 Wireless invented 1895 X-rays discovered	1894 Blackpool Tower opened
1897 Victoria's Diamond Jubilee 1899 Outbreak of Boer War 1901 Victoria dies			

Study Unit 3a: Victorian Britain

A timeline of this period includes the major events in the life and family of Queen Victoria, her marriage to Albert, and her jubilees. However, there are no sweeping changes of dynasty or civilisation as in past ages, and so the emphasis is upon industrial developments, social conditions and changes in domestic life which took place between early and late Victorian times. There are many opportunities to link local history with national events.

This is a very rich period in terms of personalities, scientific discovery and, above all, advances in such aspects of life as communication, medicine and education. These developments and discoveries are easy to represent on a timeline and may even be used to form individual thematic timelines in their own right. The lives of writers, discoverers, reformers, and inventors are useful items to chart, since knowledge of where these personalities and activities should be placed in time helps create a more precise sense of period. A chart which illustrates the social, economic, cultural and religious strands has been included here. (figure 11)

Fig 12: Time Chart for Britain since 1930

Study Unit 3b

1930s	1940s	1950s	1960s	1970s	1980s	1990s
1930: 2 million unemployed	1940: Churchill P.M.	1950: End of petrol rationing	1961: First hovercraft	1971: Decimalisation of currency	1980: 15 million cars **Traffic-free precincts built**	1990: British troops in Gulf War
1932: First Royal broadcast by George V	1940: London Blitz; Battle of Britain	1951: Festival of Britain	1962: Jamaican independence	1972: *Jesus Christ Superstar*	1980: 12 million trade union members	**High unemployment in economic recession**
1933: Adolf Hitler leads Germany	1940: Walt Disney's *Fantasia*	1952: British atomic bomb	1963: Beeching cuts railways	1973: Britain joins EEC	1981: Marriage of Charles and Diana	**Few homes without TV and video** **Increasing use of cable TV, fax machines and modems**
New industries developing **Increasing use of household appliances and synthetic fabrics** **Domestic service declines** **Increase in women workers**	1944: D-Day	1953: Edmund Hillary climbs Everest	1963: The Beatles	1973: Commercial radio	1981: Brixton riots	**'Rave' youth culture**
	1944: Education Act	1954: All food rationing ends	1964: BBC2 begins	1975: Sex Discrimination and Equal Pay Act	1982: Over 3 million unemployed **Power of trade unions weakened; membership declines**	1994: Opening of Channel tunnel
Cinema and records increasingly popular	1945: V.E. Day; Germany surrenders	**Rock 'n' roll**	1965: Death penalty abolished	1976: National Theatre opens	1982: Falklands war	1994: I.R.A. ceasefire
1936: B.B.C. launches TV service	1945: Atom bombs dropped on Japan	1955: ITV begins	1965: Churchill dies	**Return to low-level housing**	1982: Channel Four begins **More colour TVs than black and white** **Home computers**	
1936: Jarrow March	1945: *Animal Farm* published	1956: Suez crisis	**London leads world in pop and fashion; mini skirt** **Comprehensive schools**	1977: Silver Jubilee of Elizabeth II	1984: Miners' strike	
1936: Edward VIII abdicates; George VI becomes King	**New towns; tower blocks**	1956: First nuclear power station	1966: World Cup win	1978: First test tube baby born	1985: Live Aid	
Britain begins to improve defences	1946: N.H.S. Act	1956: First nuclear power station	1966: 8 million air passangers	1978: 16 million air passengers	1986: Chernobyl nuclear accident in Russia affects Britain	
1937: *The Hobbit*	1947: Railways nationalised	1957: Jodrell Bank radio telescope	1966: Colour TV	**9 million a year take foreign holidays; foreign foods become popular**	1987: Hurricane hits UK	
1939: Declaration of war	1947: Indian independence	1958: CND formed	**Fast rising wages** **TV in 10 million homes** **Foreign holidays**	1979: Margaret Thatcher first woman P.M.		
	1949: End of clothes rationing	**Large scale immigration from West Indies, India, Pakistan, E. Africa to supply labour**	1968: Race relations Act			
	1949: 1 million air passengers	**Increasing number of cars, TVs, household appliances**	1969: Discovery of North Sea oil			
	1949: Comet first jet airliner	1959: M1 motorway	1969: Concorde's first flight			
			1969: Troops sent to Northern Ireland			

Study Unit 3b: Britain Since 1930

This study unit can all too easily be dominated by the Second World War, its origins and aftermath. The period since 1930 offers many other opportunities for meaningful study, however. The twentieth century has been the age of space travel, television, computers and nuclear power. It is also the age of the private motor car, central heating and washing machine, changes which, on the surface seem trivial, but which have revolutionised the lifestyles of most ordinary people in Britain, especially those of women in the period since the Second World War.

It is possible to link personal and family histories, local and national histories in this unit. Timelines of different colours may be used and placed one above the other to show simultaneity between these different strands of history. Children can be challenged with questions about how best to represent all this information on one chart. Links with mathematics may be exploited fully here, especially with older or more able children. They can be set tasks of measuring, calculating and working out appropriate scales for complicated timelines like these. They could be asked to plan a timeline in such a way that they could show their own and their family's history on it, thus placing their personal experiences in an historical time frame. (figure 12)

Figure 13: Timeline for Study Unit 4: Ancient Greece

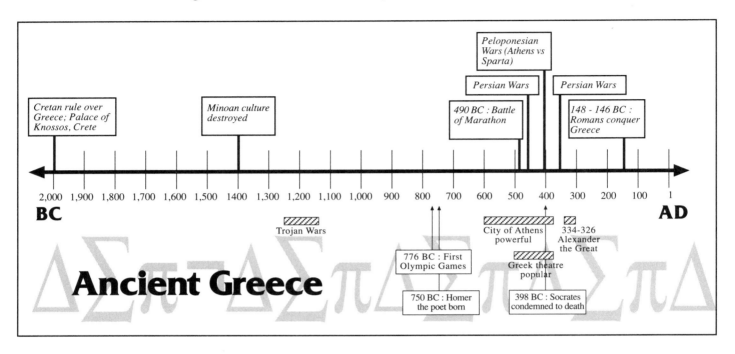

Figure 14: Timeline for Study Unit 6: Ancient Egypt

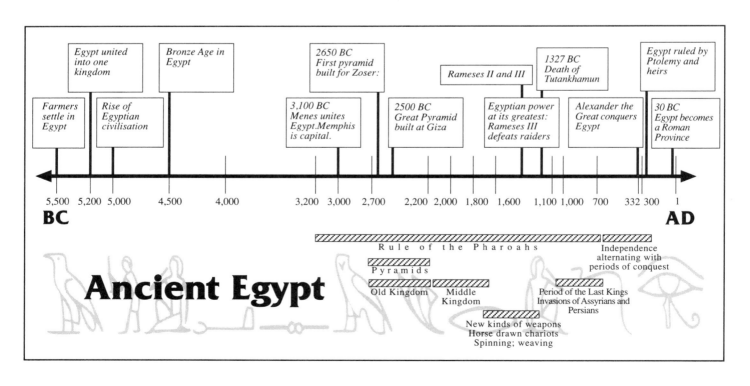

Study Unit 4: Ancient Greece

This is a challenging study unit for primary children, especially younger juniors. It is a part of history which is very remote in both time and place and it is about societies very alien to our own in many ways. Much of the published material deals with wars with other remote and, to the young child, unheard of peoples. The chronological understanding required by this period is also advanced, in that it begins many thousands of years in the past, and involves understanding and use of the terms B.C. and A.D. Aspects of Ancient Greek history which are likely to appeal to primary school children will include the early Olympic games, famous personalities, such as Archimedes, Homer and Alexander the Great, the legends, the artefacts and archaeological remains. (figure 13)

Ancient Egypt has been included here as an example of a past non-European society with temporal and political links with Ancient Greece. Important figures, such as Alexander the Great feature in both histories, as does eventual invasion and rule by Rome. (figure 14)

FIG 15: THE MAYA AND THE AZTECS
Study Unit 6

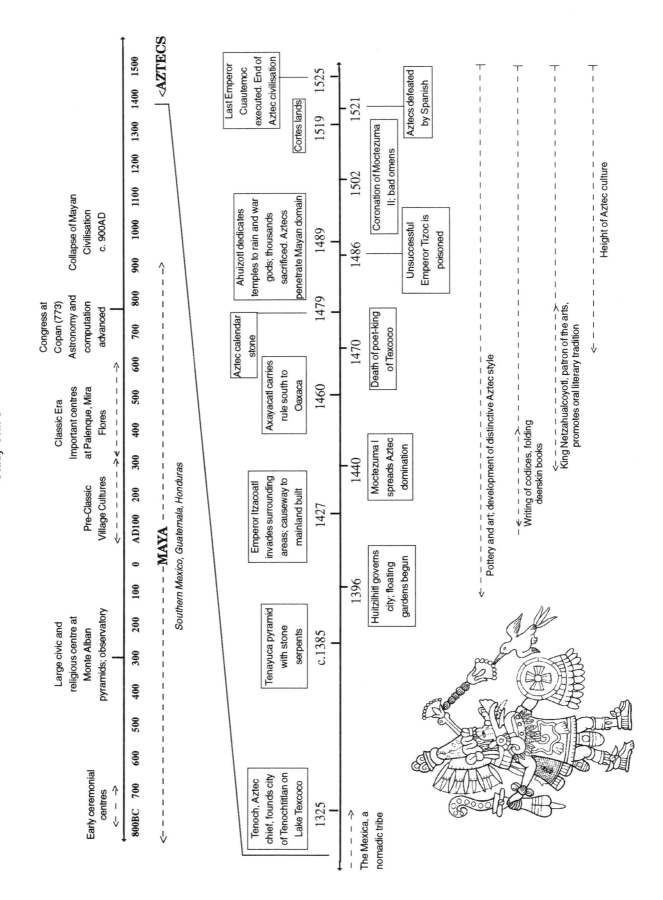

| 800BC | 700 | 600 | 500 | 400 | 300 | 200 | 100 | AD100 | 0 | 100 | 200 | 300 | 400 | 500 | 600 | 700 | 800 | 900 | 1000 | 1100 | 1200 | 1300 | 1400 | 1500 |

Early ceremonial centres

Large civic and religious centre at Monte Alban pyramids; observatory

Pre-Classic Village Cultures

Classic Era Important centres at Palenque, Mira Flores

Congress at Copan (773) Astronomy and computation advanced

Collapse of Mayan Civilisation c. 900AD

— MAYA —

Southern Mexico, Guatemala, Honduras

<AZTECS

Tenoch, Aztec chief, founds city of Tenochtitlan on Lake Texcoco
1325

The Mexica, a nomadic tribe

Tenayuca pyramid with stone serpents
c.1385

Huitzilihtl governs city; floating gardens begun
1396

Emperor Itzacoatl invades surrounding areas; causeway to mainland built
1427

Moctezuma I spreads Aztec domination
1440

Axayacatl carries rule south to Oaxaca
1460

Aztec calendar stone

Death of poet-king of Texcoco
1470

1479

Ahuizotl dedicates temples to rain and war gods; thousands sacrificed. Aztecs penetrate Mayan domain
1489

Unsuccessful Emperor Tizoc is poisoned
1486

Coronation of Moctezuma II; bad omens
1502

Cortes lands
1519

Aztecs defeated by Spanish
1521

Last Emperor Cuautemoc executed. End of Aztec civilisation
1525

Pottery and art; development of distinctive Aztec style

Writing of codices, folding deerskin books

King Netzahualcoyotl, patron of the arts, promotes oral literary tradition

Height of Aztec culture

Study Unit 6: A past non-European society - the Maya and the Aztecs

Both the Maya and the Aztecs are included in the list of non-European societies which might be selected for study. However, there are such close links between the two that it would seem logical to study the two civilisations at the same time. Both Maya and Aztecs are Central American societies, with very much the same cultural roots, religious ideologies and scholarship, with both using highly advanced systems of calculating and recording time. They had established similar social orders and produced arts and crafts of similar types. These cultures are even more remote and alien than that of the Ancient Greeks and considerable opportunity exists in their study for practising skills in interpreting archaeological evidence.

The main distinguishing feature is that Mayan civilisation pre-dated the Aztecs considerably in time, and had ceased to exist in its classical form when the Aztecs rose to power. Given that the Aztecs, at the height of their imperial power, were contemporaries of the early Tudors, it seems inaccurate to describe their culture as 'Ancient', as is often the case in published materials. It was a very different society from that in Europe at the time, rooted in a completely alien ideology, but one with numerous lasting achievements. The Aztecs had accumulated vast collections of books, known as codices, on their history, astronomy, and natural history. Their cultural and artistic skills were at their height at the time of the Conquest, with surviving pieces of sculpture prized as specimens of great artistic power in museums across the world to this day. (figure 15)

Select Resources for Teaching about Time and Timelines

GENERAL

General Series Packs and general series of books and guides have been produced by the larger publishers specifically to address the requirements of the History National Curriculum. These contain material for each of the study units. Examples of these are:

A Sense of History, general editors, James Mason and Sallie Purkis, published by the Longman Group UK Ltd, 1991-1993, revised in 1995. These materials which place considerable emphasis on teaching chronology, and can be purchased as separate items or in 'Evaluation Packs', which contain a sample of each item. There is, for each unit, a teachers' book, by Sallie Purkis, children's books, containing a variety of information and stories, posters, audio cassettes and twelve blank timelines. The teachers' books contain a wealth of suggestions for ways of using the timelines and ideas for activities based upon them. Timelines containing different types of information also appear in the children's books.

Ginn History, by the Ginn History Team, Joan Blyth, Julia Cigman, Penelope Harnett and John Sampson, published 1991-1993, indicates ways of integrating timelines and work on chronology into the study units. There are Teachers' Resources books which include photocopiable worksheets involving work on sequencing and chronology, and Pupils' Books, which include examples of timelines showing key personalities and events. The large Group Discussion Books contain much useful material for work on chronology, such as photographs of artefacts from different periods, linked with important events, and pictures of places 'then' and 'now'. There is much opportunity for discussion about change in the course using the large pictures.

Oxford Primary History for Key Stage 2, series editor, Robert Unwin, 1992-1993 also includes a variety of timelines at the beginning of each volume, with some volumes, such as 'Ancient Greece' and 'Tudors and Stuarts' looking in more detail at using and making timelines.

Collins Primary History, consists of a Teachers' Book, a Pupils' Book and a Resource Pack, containing A4 pictures of good quality. These include photographs of scenes and artefacts, which are useful for discussion and sequencing activities.

ELM have produced books and visual materials for each of the study units, *Timespan*, for KS1, by John West, and *Telltale*, for the KS2 units by John West. *Telltale* is a teachers' resource useful for story-telling.

The *Eyewitness Guides*, published by Dorling Kindersley include a wealth of detail useful as teachers' resources for work on chronology.

English Heritage produce a range of pamphlets on using primary sources and historic sites; English Heritage Education Service, Keysign House, 429 Oxford Street, London W1R 2HD.

OTHER MATERIALS AND TIMELINES

History Time-Line: Romans to Victorians, by Joan Blyth, produced by Pictorial Charts Educational Trust, (PCET) London, is a simple introductory timeline, with illustrations of key people and events. The chart is accompanied by informative notes, which suggest a variety of ways in which it might be used.

The Junior Wall Chart of History, by Christos Kondeatis, published by Studio Editions, London, 1990, covers world history from earliest times to the present and also includes explorers and traders; scientists and inventors; the arts and religion.

Timeline of the Ancient World: 300BC-AD500, by Ian Shaw, published by the British Museum Press, London 1994.

BOOKS AND PAMPHLETS

Classroom Museum, by John West, ELM, 1990, is firmly based on the author's extensive research into children's concepts of time. Chapter five, 'Children at Work' discusses activities, language use and timelines in relation to the collecting and organisation of artefacts.

Family History Patches, eds. D.J. Steel and L. Taylor (Nelson, 1978) is a series of family histories reconstructed from real evidence.

Historical Fiction in the Classroom, by V. Little and T. John, Teaching of History Series, (Historical Association, 1986) gives a comprehensive list of titles useful mainly at KS2.

Wayland's *History in Evidence* (1989) books include time charts and lists of important dates.

The BBC *Fact Finders* series (1992) has pages on 'the march of time', with useful illustrated timelines.

Face to Face (Simon and Schuster, 1992) a series of books on primary history, which have useful time charts showing durations in relation to the age of the young reader and including lists of key dates and events.

Evidence in History, Jon Nichol (Blackwell, 1982-3) contains timelines and information useful for teaching about chronology.

The Historical Association publishes a variety of pamphlets such as the *Bringing History to Life* series for KS2.

PHOTOCOPIABLE RESOURCES

Immediate History, by John Welham (Folens, 1990) includes a number of photocopiable pages dealing with timelines, sequencing, change and causation. For example, pictures of architectural details and houses from different periods are given for the child to put into chronological order.

Fulton and Simon and Schuster Education also provide similar photocopiable resources.

ARTEFACTS

Articles of Antiquity: Historical Artefacts and Resources for Education, Bury Business Centre, Kay St., Bury, Lancs BL9 6BU, sell replica artefacts.

Similar items can be purchased from *History in Evidence*, Unit 4, Holmewood Fields Business Park, Park Road, Holmewood, Chesterfield, S42 5UY, and from Past Times, Witney, Oxford, OX8 6BH.

PICTURES

Sets of A4 pictures, showing reconstructions of places, people and objects from different periods are produced by Philip Green Educational Ltd., 112a Alcester Road, Studley, Warks., B80 7NR.

Nicolas Roberts Publications have begun producing high quality A4 prints of original portraits, etchings and maps, some of which would be usable at KS1, and many at KS2. This series is called *The School's Library of Historical Source Materials*. To date, materials from the Tudor age have been produced, and others are planned.

The National Portrait Gallery have a range of Tudor portraits and a full range of the monarchs.

INFORMATION TECHNOLOGY

Time Lines, produced by Soft Teach Educational Software, is a content free computer database which has a sample timeline of British and World history but whose primary use is for older primary children to make their own timeline. There is also a Victorian Timeline.

Time Traveller, produced by E.S.M., is a computer timeline designed for use with infants, which is supplied with a sample database, but which is mainly intended for the creation of children's own timelines.

Touch Explorer Plus, a program for use with the concept keyboard, produced by the National Council for Educational Technology (NCET), includes two activities, 'Elizabethan Cottage', and 'Time Tunnel', both of which have great potential for development as part of work on chronology and 'time-placing' in connection with local studies.

Teaching History with IT, Allan M., (ed) provides a useful survey. It is published by the Historical Association, Occasional Paper No. 4, 1994.

There is also a range of materials and publications for history, produced by N.C.E.T. (National Council for Educational Technology)

SPECIAL EDUCATIONAL NEEDS

The Curriculum Council for Wales has produced some helpful material in *Teaching History to Pupils with Severe and Moderate Learning Difficulties*, (CCW, 1994)

The British Museum Education Service has produced a pack on the Ancient Civilisations for children with learning difficulties, called *Ankhs and Water Lilies*.

Big Foot, by Anne Pearson and Chitra Aloysius is a teachers' book, also produced by the British Museum Education Service (1994) about ways of using museum exhibits and large artefacts with children with severe learning difficulties. Although it refers specifically to materials in the British Museum galleries, the methodology discussed in it, such as the use of the 'sensory curriculum' is generally applicable.

History Quick Reads, by David Oakden, (Anglia Young Books, 1994) are written for children with special educational needs, and cover most KS2 periods.

ADDITIONAL MATERIALS FOR KS1

There are suggestions for activities to develop progression in children's sense of chronology in chapter four of *Teaching History at Key Stage 1*, NCC, 1993

There are childrens' books in the *Starting History* packs, Scholastic Publications, and the *Changing Times* series, Franklin Watts.

Picture and story books which introduce notions of time include:

Mr. Wolf's Week, Colin Hawkins

Seasons, John Burningham

My Great Grandpa, Martin Waddell and Don Mansell

The Patchwork Quilt, Valerie Flournoy

Grandma's Bill, Martin Waddell

Shaker Lane, Alice and Martin Provensen

Jack at Sea, Philippe Dupasquier

Stories for Time: Resourcing the History Curriculum for KS1, and *More Stories for Time: Resourcing the History Curriculum for KS2 and KS3*, by Chris Routh and Anne Rowe (University of Reading, Reading and Language Information Centre, 1992) give further titles.

Examples of illustrated books which provide visual knowledge of a period include the Beatrix Potter books, Orlando the Marmalade Cat and the Paddington Bear books.

ADDITIONAL MATERIALS FOR KS2 STUDY UNITS

Select resources for study units mentioned in the text.

ROMANS, ANGLO-SAXONS AND VIKINGS IN BRITAIN

The Agricola, by Tacitus, (Penguin, 1948). Accounts of life in Roman Britain.

A Guide to Roman Remains in Britain, R.J.A. Wilson

Anglo-Saxon Chronicles, by Anne Savage (Heinemann, 1982)

There are various versions of Beowulf, such as those by Rosemary Sutcliff (Bodley, 1961) and Robert Nye (Beaver, 1985)

Anglo-Saxons by John Fines and Tony Hopkins, (Historical Association Pamphlet, 1993)

The Sutton Hoo Ship Burial, British Museum Education Service.

The Vikings, by John Fines (1992) is an Historical Association pamphlet which includes extracts from the Viking saga books, very useful for first hand evidence of what life was like in Viking times.

The Vikings, BBC television Zig Zag series.

The Time Traveller Book of Viking Raiders, A. Civardi and J. Graham-Campbell (Usborne, 1977)

The Vikings, a computer simulation of Viking raids, in the form of a decision-making game, produced by Fernleaf.

Invaders and Settlers, a timeline by PCET designed to provide an outline of the Roman, Anglo-Saxon and Viking invasions, conveniently divided into the three corresponding sections. Activities based on place names are suggested in the notes.

LIFE IN TUDOR TIMES

History 5-11: Tudors and Stuarts, BBC 1991-2. Five television broadcasts with teachers' notes.

Timelines: Tudors and Stuarts a Channel Four Educational Television series on life in the 16th and 17th centuries (Spring, 1992).

Tudor and Stuart Timeline, by Dr Robert Unwin, (PCET,1993) designed to support the Channel Four series, referred to above. Key events and changes in society, technology, science, literature and architecture are shown above and below the line.

Kingdom of Benin Timeline, from PCET, produced to support the Channel 4 Schools Programme, Benin: An African Kingdom, shows parallels between the Kingdom of Benin at its height and Tudor and Stuart Britain. It is a useful resource for linking a non- European study unit with the Tudors.

VICTORIAN BRITAIN

The *How We Used to Live* series, published by A & C Black, accompanies the Yorkshire Television programmes. It contains a useful volume on *Victorians, Early and Late*, by David Evans, (1990) which includes a time chart of the period divided into decades.

Could do Better, from Charlotte Mason College, Low Nook, Ambleside, LA22 9RB, is a collection of original source materials on the subject of school life.

The Victorians Timeline, Soft Teach Educational Software (1991), Sturgess Farmhouse, Longbridge Deverill, Warminster, Wilts. BA12 7EA.

BRITAIN SINCE 1930

History Time-line: Twentieth Century, by Joan Blyth (PCET, 1994) is designed to provide a chronological framework for this study unit.

How We Used To Live, (1954-1970) videos, computer programs and books. (A & C Black, in conjunction with Yorkshire TV, to accompany broadcasts of the same title.)

Ancient Greece

Childhood in the Greek and Roman World and *A Visit to the Ancient Olympic Games*, Videos from the British Museum Education Service.

The Joint Association of Classical Teachers, 31-34 Gordon Square, London, WC1H 0PY, has pamphlets, booklists and local contacts.

Ancient Egypt

Usbourne Time Traveller: Pharaohs and Pyramids, Allan, A., (Usbourne, 1977)

Landmarks, BBC schools broadcast, summer 1991

Ancient Egypt, (PCET, 1994)

The Aztecs

The Broken Spears: the Aztec Account of the Conquest of Mexico, by Miguel Leon-Portilla, (Beacon, 1962) contains original text and illustrations from the Florentine Codex, telling the story of the Conquest from the perspective of the indigenous peoples.

What do we know about the Aztecs?, by Joanna Defrates (Simon and Schuster, 1991) contains an excellent timeline comparing the time of the Aztecs with contemporary developments in Europe, Asia and Africa.

Ancient America: Cultural Atlas for Young People, by Marion Wood (Equinox, 1990) is a general reference book for teachers or very able older juniors, covering the whole of early American history. However it provides a useful 'table of dates' which shows the relationships in time between different societies, particularly the Maya and Aztecs, both of which are Mexican cultures. It also places these histories geographically and gives much contextual information about these geographical areas and their peoples in the present day, so that both continuity and change may be seen.

Teaching about the Aztecs: A Cross-Curricular Perspective, By Angela Horton, (Historical Association Pamphlet P4. 1992)

Notes and References

1. Piaget, J., *The Child's Conception of Time* (Routledge, 1967) Trans. by A.J. Pomerans. This was first published in French in 1927.

2. See, for example, von Franz, M.L., *Time: Rhythm and Repose*, (Thames and Hudson, 1978)

3. The double helix was discovered to be the basic structure of deoxyribonucleic acid (DNA) by James Watson and Francis Crick in 1953. This molecular structure is thought to be the basis of heredity.

4. Various methods of measuring time in different cultures are discussed in an informative article by Jahoda, G., "Children's Concepts of Time and History" (*Educational Review* 15, 1963)

5. Piaget, J., op. cit.

6. *History in the National Curriculum* (DfE/HMSO, 1995)

7. This issue is discussed in Lomas, T., *Teaching and Assessing Historical Understanding*, (Historical Association Teaching of History Series 63, 1993 edition)

8. Piaget, J., op. cit.

9. Jahoda, G., op. cit.

10. Levstik, L. S. and Pappas, C., "Exploring the Development of Historical Understanding" (*Journal of Research and Development in Education* 21, 1987)

11. Vygotsky, L.S., *Thought and Language*, (MIT Press, 1962)

12. Donaldson, M., *Childen's Minds*, (Collins, 1978)

13. Bryant, P. E., *Perception and Understanding in Young Children*, (Methuen, 1974)

14. Bruner, J.S., *Beyond the Information Given*, (Allen and Unwin, 1973)

15. Fraisse, P., "The Adaptation of the Child to Time" in Friedman, W.J. (ed) *The Developmental Psychology of Time*, (Academic Press, 1982)

16. Friedman, W.J., *The Developmental Psychology of Time*, (Academic Press, 1982)

17. West, J., *History 7 - 13*, (Dudley Metropolitan Borough) 1981, p.6

18. The findings of this study are discussed in West, J., "Time Charts", (*Education* 3 - 13, 1981)

19. Blyth, J., *History in Primary Schools: A Practical Approach for Teachers of 5-11 Year old Children*, (Open University Press, 1989); *History 5 to 11*, (Hodder and Stoughton, 1994)

20. Levstik and Pappas, op. cit.

21. Cooper, H., *The Teaching of History*, (Fulton, 1992)

22. See articles by Wood, Simchowitz and Hodkinson, in *Teaching History*, (April 1995)

23. *English in the National Curriculum*, (DfE/HMSO, 1995)

24. D.E.S. , *A Language for Life* (The Bullock Report), (HMSO, 1975)

25. Bruner, J.S., *The Process of Education*, (Vintage, 1960)

26. Beard, R., "An Investigation into Concept Formation among Infant School Children" (PhD. thesis, Univ of London, 1957)

27. West, J., op.cit.

28. Tough, J., *The Development of Meaning*, (Unwin, 1977)

29. Blyth, J. (1994), op. cit.

30. History stories, such as Boudicca, Mary Seacole and the Mayflower, part of the Ginn History Materials.

31. "Elizabeth I" broadcast in the Watch series (BBC, 1994?)

32. *Moving Memories*, a series of documentary videotapes, produced by the North West Film Archive (Manchester Metropolitan University)

33. Hoodless, P., "Language Use and Problem Solving in Primary History", (*Teaching History*, June 1994)

34. Davies, J., "Time Walk", (*Child Education*, June 1990)

35. West, J., *Classroom Museum*, (ELM, 1990)

36. See, for example, Hoodless, P., "A Victorian Case Study: Simulating Aspects of Victorian Life in the Classroom", (*Primary History*, June, 1994)

37. Madeley, H., *Time Charts*, (Historical Association Pamphlet No.50, 1921)

38. Pictorial Charts Educational Trust, London

39. *Non-Statutory Guidance for Northern Ireland*, (CCNI,1991)

40. *Final Order and Non-Statutory Guidance for Wales*, (CCW, 1991)

41. *Teaching History at Key Stage 1*, (NCC, 1993)

42. Johnson, P., *A Book of One's Own: Developing Literacy through Making Books*, (Hodder and Stoughton, 1990)

43. *Time Lines*, an I.T. program produced by Soft Teach Educational Software

44. Scarre, C., *Timelines of the Ancient World: a Visual Chronology from the Origins of Life to AD 1500*, (Dorling Kindersley, 1993)

45. A poster and booklet are produced by the SHAP Working Party (SHAP, 1994)

46. Blyth, J., (1994), op.cit.

Select Bibliography

Blyth, J., *History in Primary Schools: A Practical Approach for Teachers of 5 - 11 Year old Children*, (Open University Press, 1989)

Blyth, J., *History 5-11*, (Hodder and Stoughton, 1994)

Chapman, G. and Robson, P., *Exploring Time*, (Simon and Schuster, 1994)

Cooper, H., *The Teaching of History*, (Fulton, 1992)

Donaldson, M., *Children's Minds*, (Collins, 1978)

Johnson, P., *A Book of One's Own: Developing Literacy through Making Books* (Hodder and Stoughton, 1990)

Lomas, T., *Teaching and Assessing Historical Understanding*, (Historical Association, Teaching of History Series, No. 63, 1989)

Pluckrose, H., *Children Learning History*, (Blackwell, 1991)

Routh, C. and Rowe, A., *Stories for Time; More Stories for Time*, (University of Reading, 1992)

Scarre, C., *Timelines of the Ancient World: A Visual Chronology from the Origins of Life to A.D. 1500*m (Dorling Kindersley, 1993)

Unwin, R., *The Visual Dimension in the Study of History*, (Historical Association, Teaching of History Series, No. 49, 1981)

von Franz, M., Time: *Rhythm and Repose*, (Thames and Hudson, 1978)

West, J., *History 7 - 13*, (Dudley Metropolitan Borough, 1981)

West, J., *Classroom Museum*, (Elm, 1990)